CATS SET IV

SPHYNX CATS

Nancy Furstinger
ABDO Publishing Company

visit us at
www.abdopub.com

Published by ABDO Publishing Company, 4940 Viking Drive, Edina, Minnesota 55435.
Copyright © 2006 by Abdo Consulting Group, Inc. International copyrights reserved in
all countries. No part of this book may be reproduced in any form without written
permission from the publisher. The Checkerboard Library™ is a trademark and logo of
ABDO Publishing Company.

Printed in the United States.

Cover Photo: Peter Arnold
Interior Photos: Animals Animals pp. 13, 15, 17, 20; Corbis pp. 4, 5, 7, 19;
    Ron Kimball pp. 9, 11, 21

Series Coordinator: Megan Murphy
Editors: Stephanie Hedlund, Megan Murphy
Art Direction: Neil Klinepier

Library of Congress Cataloging-in-Publication Data

Furstinger, Nancy.
    Sphynx cats / Nancy Furstinger.
        p. cm. -- (Cats. Set IV)
    Includes bibliographical references.
    ISBN 1-59679-269-8
        1. Sphynx cat--Juvenile literature. I. Title.

SF449.S68.F87 2005
636.8--dc22
                                                                    2005043337

CONTENTS

LIONS, TIGERS, AND CATS

Around 3,500 years ago, people in Egypt tamed African wildcats. These cats hunted rats and mice that feasted on crops stored in granaries. Ancient people worshipped cats. They believed these animals brought prosperity and good fortune.

Domestic cats are related to these African wildcats. Today, people cherish cats as precious family

The Great Sphinx of Egypt has the head of a man and the body of a lion. This monument is evidence of the cat's sacred place in ancient times.

4

This lynx kitten shares many similarities with kittens in domestic cat breeds. But unlike house cats, wildcats cannot purr.

members. More than 40 different **breeds** of **domestic** cats exist.

All cats belong to the **Felidae** family. This family contains 38 different species, including lions, tigers, and clouded leopards. All cats share similar **traits**. They stalk prey using sharp teeth and claws. And whether big or small, they all enjoy catnapping!

SPHYNX CATS

Hairless cats are not a new **phenomenon**. Hundreds of years ago, the Aztec people of South America **bred** hairless cats. More recently, a breed known as the Mexican hairless appeared in North America.

Throughout history, furry cats have randomly given birth to hairless kittens. These kittens are considered a quirk of nature. Hairless kittens appear in **litters** around the world.

The sphynx breed we know today was a Canadian discovery. In 1966, a black-and-white short-haired cat in Canada gave birth to a hairless kitten. A modern breeding program was started to establish this hairless **mutation** in a cat line.

Other names for the sphynx cat include the Canadian hairless and the moon cat. It has also been called *le chat sans poils*, which is French for "the naked cat." The **Cat Fanciers' Association** recognized the sphynx as a **breed** in 1998.

This cat was named after the Great Sphinx in Egypt.

QUALITIES

The sphynx **breed** is lively and intelligent. This cat bursts with energy and loves to run and climb. Sometimes its curiosity leads to mischief. But its sweet, affectionate nature will never let you stay angry for long.

This breed will often entertain you. The sphynx will perform silly tricks and check to make certain you are watching. This attitude makes the sphynx a terrific show cat.

The sphynx is a champion cuddler. Due to its lack of fur, this cat seeks out warmth. It will often slip between the bedsheets to snuggle.

Sphynx need a lot of attention to keep them happy. They may become depressed if they feel lonely. So, they should never be left alone for long periods of time.

Your sphynx will appreciate having another cat or companion to play with.

COAT AND COLOR

At first glance, the sphynx cat always causes a reaction. People are either charmed by its appearance, or put off by it. However, the sphynx's loving personality usually wins people over.

Sphynx are not completely hairless. Soft, fuzzy down covers their wrinkled skin. Short, fine hairs also coat the cat's nose, toes, and ears. A tiny puff may tip the tail. If it has whiskers at all, they are short and few.

These cats feel like a fuzzy peach or warm suede. Their bodies are unusually warm despite their lack of hair. They do shed their downy fur. However, they don't have to worry about hair balls!

This unusual **breed** comes in almost every color. The color you see is the skin color along with the small amount of hairs on the coat. Like humans, these cats can sunburn.

SIZE

The sphynx is a medium-sized cat with a long, muscular body. Males weigh from 8 to 11 pounds (4 to 5 kg). Females are usually lighter, weighing 6 to 8 pounds (3 to 4 kg).

This cat has a broad chest and a barrel-shaped body. It should have a bit of a belly, as if it just finished a meal. Its paws have unusually long toes and thick pads. The whiplike tail tapers toward the tip.

The sphynx has a friendly, intelligent face. Its head is wedge shaped, and it has large, batlike ears set high on its head. The sphynx also has large, lemon-shaped eyes.

Opposite page: The sphynx is a sturdy cat, even though its hairlessness makes it look small compared to other cat breeds.

CARE

This hairless cat requires more grooming than many furry **breeds**. The sphynx is the only cat with sweat glands. When the cat sweats, it produces oil. The sphynx doesn't have fur to absorb the oil. So its skin can become greasy.

The sphynx needs to be bathed at least every two weeks. If accustomed to baths as a kitten, your sphynx will actually come to enjoy its bath time. And, drying the sphynx takes only seconds!

Your sphynx needs a warm spot to snuggle year-round. Toys will keep this active breed entertained for hours. Like all cats, the sphynx also needs a **litter box** to bury its waste. Keep the box in a low-traffic area away from its food and water.

Bring your sphynx to a veterinarian for a yearly checkup and **vaccines**. The veterinarian can also **spay** or **neuter** your pet.

The sphynx's big ears also need cleaning. Without ear hair, dust and dirt cannot be filtered.

FEEDING

When you take your sphynx home, feed it the same food that it is used to eating. Later, you can slowly change brands by mixing in new food. This will prevent your cat from getting an upset stomach.

Unlike some other cat **breeds**, the sphynx isn't picky about what it eats. Instead, it has a raging appetite. This cat will eat more than most. Sometimes, the sphynx will even try to steal food!

Along with treats, feed your cat a balanced diet. Protein, such as fish, should be on the daily menu. Serve food and fresh water in stainless steel bowls. While many kittens crave milk, some adult cats are unable to digest it.

*The sprlight sometimes uses its toes as fingers!
It may use these toes when eating or playing.*

KITTENS

Sphynx cats are loving mothers. They are **pregnant** for about 63 to 65 days. A typical **litter** has three to four kittens. All kittens are blind and deaf at birth.

Sphynx kittens are born with very wrinkled skin. But, most of their wrinkles will disappear as they grow. However, some wrinkling is desirable in this **breed**.

Sphynx kittens show their intelligence early. They usually open their eyes within two or three days. And, they can start eating solid food by three weeks of age. By the time they are 12 weeks old, the kittens can join their new families.

Sphynx kittens are usually fuzzy balls of wrinkles!

BUYING A KITTEN

A healthy sphynx can live 18 years or more. This **breed** is hearty with few health problems. But it demands a lot of attention, so make sure you are ready for a lifelong responsibility.

The sphynx is rather rare. If this breed has captured your heart, be patient. Most sphynx breeders have long waiting lists for their kittens.

If you are allergic to cat fur, you might be able to live with a sphynx. However, many people

Sphynx are typically very loud cats. Many people say they even exceed the Siamese in volume. Siamese cats are considered one of the most vocal breeds.

are actually affected by **dander**. Spend some time around a sphynx before you adopt one. While you wait, you can seek out the most playful, active kitten to become your new best friend!

Because of their affectionate and active natures, sphynx have been described as "part cat, part dog, part monkey, and part child."

GLOSSARY

breed - a group of animals sharing the same appearance and characteristics. A breeder is a person who raises animals. Raising animals is often called breeding them.

Cat Fanciers' Association (CFA) - a group that sets the standards for judging all breeds of cats.

dander - saliva that dries on the skin or coat when cats groom themselves.

domestic - animals that are tame.

Felidae - the scientific Latin name for the cat family.

litter - all of the kittens born at one time to a mother cat.

litter box - a box filled with cat litter, which is similar to sand. Cats use litter boxes to dispose of their waste.

mutation - a distinct change in the genes of a human, a plant, or an animal.

neuter (NOO-tuhr) - to remove a male animal's reproductive organs.

phenomenon (fih-NAH-muh-nahn) - something that is rare or exceptional.

pregnant - having one or more babies growing within the body.

spay - to remove a female animal's reproductive organs.

trait - a quality that distinguishes one person or group from another.

vaccine (vak-SEEN) - a shot given to animals or humans to prevent them from getting an illness or disease.

WEB SITES

To learn more about sphynx cats, visit ABDO Publishing Company on the World Wide Web at **www.abdopub.com**. Web sites about these cats are featured on our Book Links page. These links are routinely monitored and updated to provide the most current information available.

INDEX